Gun Education and Safety

GUN HISTORY & DEVELOPMENT

BRIAN KEVIN

ABDO Publishing Company

visit us at
www.abdopublishing.com

Published by ABDO Publishing Company, PO Box 398166, Minneapolis, MN 55439.
Copyright © 2012 by Abdo Consulting Group, Inc. International copyrights reserved in all
countries. No part of this book may be reproduced in any form without written permission from the
publisher. The Checkerboard Library™ is a trademark and logo of ABDO Publishing Company.

Printed in the United States of America, North Mankato, Minnesota.
112011
012012

Cover Photo: Getty Images
Interior Photos: Alamy pp. 5, 15, 16, 18–19, 19, 24; AP Images pp. 12, 17, 20–21;
    Getty Images p. 6; Glow Images p. 14; iStockphoto pp. 24–25; Special thanks to Kristi Geyer
    p. 29; National Geographic Stock p. 9; North Wind Picture Archives p. 11; Photolibrary p. 13;
    Thinkstock pp. 22, 23, 27; Photo Courtesy of U.S. Army p. 26; Wikimedia Commons p. 8

Series Coordinator: Megan M. Gunderson
Editors: Megan M. Gunderson, BreAnn Rumsch
Art Direction: Neil Klinepier

Library of Congress Cataloging-in-Publication Data

Kevin, Brian, 1980-
 Gun history & development / Brian Kevin.
    p. cm. -- (Gun education and safety)
 Includes index.
 ISBN 978-1-61783-314-4
 1. Firearms--History--Juvenile literature. I. Title. II. Title: Gun history and development.
 TS533.K48 2012
 683.4--dc23
                        2011031411

CONTENTS

Black Berthold 4

Black Powder 6

Big Cannons 8

Hand Cannons. 10

The Arquebus 12

Muskets 14

Rifles. 16

Pistols and Revolvers 18

Ammunition 20

Manufacturing 24

Modern Guns 26

Gun Rights 28

Glossary 30

Web Sites 31

Index. 32

Black Berthold

   Black Berthold was a German monk who lived in the 1300s. He was also an alchemist, a scientist who experiments with metals and chemicals. At the time, these scientists worked to turn natural materials into valuable substances. Some even thought they could turn common metals into gold!

   One day, Black Berthold combined saltpeter, charcoal, and sulfur. He mixed the three chemicals together with a **mortar and pestle**. Suddenly, there was a loud noise and a bright flash! Black Berthold jumped away as the pestle shot out of the mortar.

   Black Berthold realized that the chemicals had created the explosion. Combined together, they made black powder. This would be the first material used as gunpowder.

   Black Berthold's experience inspired him. He decided to combine the three chemicals in a long, closed tube. They would shoot a **projectile** out of the tube, just as his pestle had shot out of the mortar. In addition to discovering black powder, Black Berthold invented the very first gun.

Little is known of Black Berthold's life.

Black Powder

Roger Bacon also studied languages. He may have learned about black powder by reading Arabic texts.

The story of Black Berthold is a myth. He was a real person named Berthold Schwarz. But no one really knows how black powder was invented. Scholars believe that over time, many people helped to develop it.

More than 1,000 years ago in China, people used black powder to make fireworks and signals. This early gunpowder might have been used in India even before that.

All the ingredients were available there. This may be where Middle Eastern traders picked up their supplies. From there, black powder spread into Europe.

The first European to write down a formula for black powder was another monk. Roger Bacon studied many things, including math and alchemy. In 1242, he wrote down careful instructions for making black powder.

GUNPOWDER

Early weapons were only as strong as the person using them. The invention of gunpowder changed that. Gunpowder is an explosive, fast-burning material used to propel ammunition out of weapons.

The first material used as gunpowder was black powder. It was used in the earliest guns right up through the 1800s. Eventually, it was replaced by smokeless powder.

This new type of gunpowder creates less smoke and flash than black powder. And, it is easier to control how fast the powder burns. It is common in firearms today.

Not just any combination of the ingredients will work. There has to be exactly the right amount of each for the powder to **ignite**. Bacon had determined the correct mixture.

To keep his formula a secret, Bacon wrote it down in Latin using a special code. Still, it didn't take long for this knowledge to spread.

Big Cannons

The earliest known picture of a gun is from 1326.

In the 1300s, Europeans adopted black powder for use in firearms. Some of the very first firearms were huge, heavy cannons. These early guns had important elements that are still found in modern guns.

One main piece was the barrel. This is the long tube that a **projectile** is fired out of. Many early cannon barrels were made of metals such as bronze or cast iron.

The earliest cannons had huge, rounded back ends. So, they looked like tipped-over vases. Later cannons were straighter.

The base was another key part. Since cannons were so large and heavy, they couldn't be held by a person. Instead they were supported by a base.

To fire a cannon, the user poured black powder into the open front end of the barrel. Next, an arrow or a stone ball went in.

At the back of the barrel was a smaller hole called a touchhole. Through this hole, the user lit the black powder with a special match or a red-hot iron.

The force of the exploding powder shot the **projectile** out of the barrel. By the late 1300s, cannons could fire stone balls weighing more than 450 pounds (200 kg)!

The word cannon *comes from the Latin word* canna, *which means "tube" or "reed."*

Hand Cannons

Big, heavy cannons were difficult to move and aim. So, people also used smaller cannons that fit in a person's hand. These had been in use since the mid-1200s in China. There, black powder shot stone **projectiles** out of bamboo barrels. Around 1300, Arabs used a handheld gun made of bamboo and metal. It relied on black powder to fire an arrow.

The small firearms developed in Europe had metal barrels. These early hand cannons were loaded in the same way as large cannons. The black powder and projectile went in through the **muzzle**. Then, the user lit the powder. He used a hot wire poker or a slow-burning match, or fuse. This reached the powder through a touchhole at the back end of the barrel.

Still, hand cannons were clumsy. A person had to hold the cannon at one end and light the powder with the other hand. Sometimes, the process took two people. All of this made it difficult to aim **accurately**.

Yet gun makers did not give up on handheld guns. They worked to improve this important tool. Soon, armies everywhere relied on their power.

Hand cannons weren't just difficult to aim. They also took time to reload.

The Arquebus

During the 1400s, handheld guns became more advanced. One gun that represented these important improvements was the arquebus.

Arquebuses were different from cannons because the black powder was not lit by hand. Instead, there was an S-shaped clamp at the back of the barrel. This held a lit match.

On the side of the gun was a pan. It contained a small amount of black powder called priming powder, or primer. A trail of primer led from the pan into the gun's barrel. Like hand cannons, this is where the main powder and **projectile** sat.

When the gunman pulled the trigger, the match fell onto the pan. The match lit the primer. This **ignited** the powder inside the barrel to fire a round bullet.

An arquebus is also called a harquebus or a hackbut.

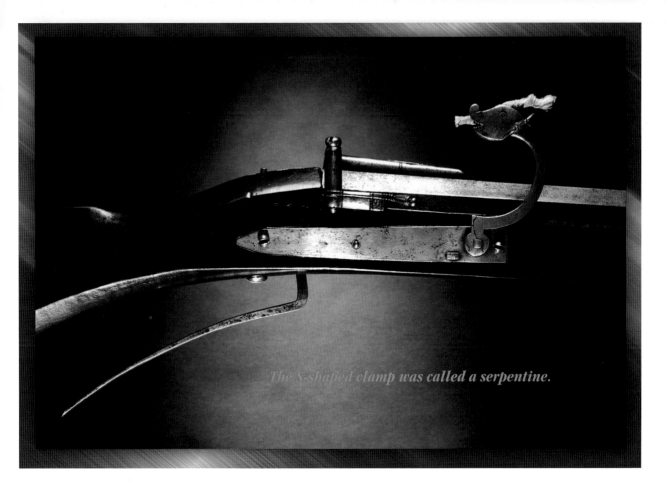

The S-shaped clamp was called a serpentine.

    With this matchlock system, the gunman could hold an arquebus with two hands. This made the gun easier to aim.

    The arquebus also changed how guns were held. Before, shooters braced them against the chest or the side of the body. Now, they began holding them up to the shoulder. The arquebus remained popular until it was replaced by the musket.

Muskets

The musket was a larger version of the arquebus. It was developed in the 1500s. Early versions had to be propped up by a support stick. Even so, muskets became popular with European armies.

However, the early musket's operation was not ideal. It was another matchlock gun. It was hard to keep the match lit during battle, especially in wind or rain. Also, the flame's light could reveal an army's position to the enemy. Soldiers needed a gun that didn't require a lit match to fire.

So, Italian gun makers

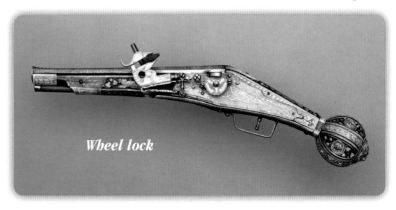

Wheel lock

invented the wheel lock firing **mechanism**. It consisted of a metal wheel that turned when a shooter pulled the trigger. The wheel scraped against a piece of iron pyrite to produce sparks. The sparks lit the gunpowder, so a match

flint

frizzen

stock

pan

barrel

trigger

Flintlock

was no longer needed to fire the gun. Yet wheel locks were expensive. More improvement was needed.

Next, gun makers invented a **mechanism** that held a piece of flint. Pulling the trigger caused the flint to scrape against a piece of steel, or frizzen. This produced the sparks needed to fire the gun. This was a key development. Flintlocks remained popular for the next 200 years.

Rifles

Gun makers didn't only improve how guns were fired. They also invented new ways for a bullet to leave the barrel. The inside of early musket and cannon barrels was smooth. So, these were called smoothbore guns.

In the 1400s, Austrian gunsmith Gaspard Kollner began to carve spiral grooves along the inside of his gun barrels. This

Rifled barrels are common in rifles, handguns, and cannons.

Modern rifles are often loaded near the back of the barrel.

is called rifling. The grooves caused the bullet to spin as it traveled through the air, like a football. The spinning motion improved the bullet's **accuracy**.

At this time, most bullets were plain lead balls. It was difficult to fit them tightly into a rifle. They had to be rammed down the barrel, which took much time.

So in the early 1500s, some gun makers started creating a new style of gun. These had an opening at the breech, or back of the barrel. The bullet and powder could be loaded there. Breech-loading rifles became popular in the 1800s. Modern soldiers and sportsmen still use this type of gun.

Meanwhile, guns with smooth bores remained popular for hunting birds. These "fowling pieces" could be loaded with many tiny metal pellets called shot. The shot spread out when fired. Over time, these guns led to modern shotguns. Today, they remain popular among bird hunters.

Pistols and Revolvers

Early design improvements had made guns easier to use and aim. Yet they were still large weapons.

So in the mid-1400s, inventors also began developing handguns. By the early 1500s, these pistols could only shoot a few feet. And, it took time to reload them between each shot. So, horse riders carried more than one at a time!

Gun makers addressed this design problem in two ways. Some built guns with multiple barrels. Others created guns with multiple cylinders. These held the **projectiles**, which shot out of just one barrel. Either way, these revolvers could be fired more than once without reloading.

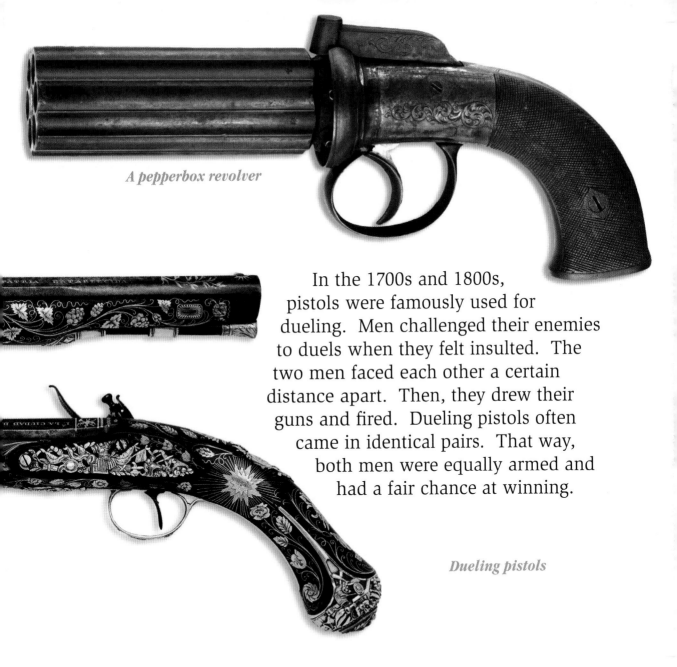

A pepperbox revolver

In the 1700s and 1800s, pistols were famously used for dueling. Men challenged their enemies to duels when they felt insulted. The two men faced each other a certain distance apart. Then, they drew their guns and fired. Dueling pistols often came in identical pairs. That way, both men were equally armed and had a fair chance at winning.

Dueling pistols

Ammunition

Guns weren't the only thing that went through many changes. The objects being fired out of them also had room for improvement.

The earliest cannons mostly used balls of stone or iron. Bullets for early handheld guns were small lead balls.

These round bullets were fine for smoothbore firearms. But they didn't work well in rifles. To spin in the rifled barrel, the balls had to fit snugly. This made the guns difficult to load.

In 1823, British Army captain John Norton invented a pointed bullet. It had a hollow base that expanded under pressure. So, it slid in easily when loading the gun. Then when the gun was fired, the pressure of the explosion expanded the base to fit the barrel.

Black powder and a lead ball for a flintlock musket

Gunmen were always concerned with how quickly they could reload their weapons. In early guns, shooters had to load the bullet, gunpowder, and primer separately. Sometimes, the powder was kept in a flask. Other times, it was stored in small paper cartridges. These were ripped open and poured down the barrel.

To simplify these steps, gun makers started developing cartridges that held both the powder and the bullet. These new containers were made of metal. They were related to percussion locks. This new type of firing system followed flintlocks.

With the new lock, the trigger released a small hammer. The hammer struck

Modern rifle and handgun cartridges have four main parts. A case contains priming powder at the bottom and gunpowder in the middle. A bullet is on top.

a percussion cap. This released primer in the cap, which **ignited** the gunpowder in the barrel.

In the mid-1850s, centerfire cartridges were finally introduced. These sealed brass cases contained a percussion cap, powder, and a bullet. When the shooter pulled the trigger, a pin hit the thin base of the case. This set off the explosion necessary to shoot the bullet. The centerfire cartridge is still popular today.

In a shotgun shell, a wad of paper separates the primer and gunpowder from the shot.

Manufacturing

For hundreds of years, guns were made one at a time. A specialized craftsman made each part. Some metalworkers made the barrels. Others created the pieces for each lock individually. Woodworkers carved the stocks. Some guns were beautifully decorated. And being handmade, each one was different from the next.

American inventor Samuel Colt created the first successful repeating pistol in 1835. His six-shooters became famous in the West.

Some early guns were works of art and technology.

In Europe and the United States, some areas became known for gun making. Birmingham, England, was famous for its Gun Quarter. Brescia, Italy, produced a specific type of gun decoration. Gunsmith Bartolomeo Beretta started making barrels in Venice, Italy, in 1526. His company still exists today!

In the 1800s, the **Industrial Revolution** changed how guns were made. New machines could make many identical gun parts all at once. Suddenly, gun parts were interchangeable.

Gun making soon became a major industry. US companies built large factories. They sold guns and ammunition to armies, police, and sportsmen around the world.

In the mid-1800s, many guns were needed for wars in the United States and Europe. High demand made gun manufacturers very successful. Colt, Smith & Wesson, and Remington are famous American companies from that time. They all still produce guns today.

Modern Guns

The US Army's M-249 Squad Automatic Weapon fires 750 rounds per minute.

In the 1890s, firearms maker John Moses Browning made a leap forward in gun design. He designed semiautomatic guns. Like other guns, they fired one shot for every trigger pull. However, semiautomatic weapons reload themselves after being fired.

Fully automatic weapons became popular in the 1900s. These guns reload and fire continuously while the trigger is pulled. They are also known as machine guns.

The most famous early automatic weapon was the Thompson submachine gun, or "tommy gun." American gangsters like John Dillinger and Al Capone used tommy guns in the early 1900s.

Some modern sights improve aim by making a target appear closer. Silencers fit on the front end of the barrel to make the gun quieter.

Tommy guns were also important tools for soldiers during **World War I**. In fact, the invention of automatic guns changed warfare forever. Suddenly, guns were far deadlier than ever before.

Developments continued with silencers and improved sights. These and other advances have made guns quieter and more **accurate**.

Gun Rights

The history of guns is connected to the history of the United States. Many of America's Founding Fathers didn't want the new country to have a single, standing army. They wanted free men to have their own weapons. That way, the men could be ready to fight if needed. And, they would be free to arm themselves against tyrants.

In 1788, the US **Constitution** went into effect. Three years later, leaders added ten **amendments** called the Bill of Rights. The Second Amendment states, "A well regulated **Militia**, being necessary to the security of a free State, the right of the people to keep and bear Arms, shall not be infringed."

Today, people disagree about what this means. Some believe it means the army should have the right to bear arms. Others believe it also gives the right to bear arms to the people. Both sides have been argued in many court cases.

Today, representatives of the two sides work to influence gun laws. Groups such as the National Rifle Association support fewer restrictions on gun ownership. Groups such as the Coalition to Stop Gun Violence argue for more control.

The story of guns continues with each new development and law. Understanding the history of guns helps us make informed decisions about gun rights. Certainly old Black Berthold would never have expected so much from his accidental explosion!

People have felt strongly about gun rights for hundreds of years. Understanding the history of guns will help you decide how you feel about gun rights.

GLOSSARY

accurate - free of errors.

amendment - a change to a country's or a state's constitution.

Constitution - the laws that govern the United States.

ignite - to set on fire.

Industrial Revolution - a period in England from about 1750 to 1850. It marked the change from an agricultural to an industrial society.

mechanism - a system of parts working together.

militia (muh-LIH-shuh) - an army of citizens trained for emergencies and national defense.

mortar and pestle (PEH-suhl) - a mortar is a strong bowl in which a substance is pounded. This is done with a club-shaped tool called a pestle.

muzzle - the open front end of the barrel of a weapon.

projectile - an object that can be thrown or shot out.

World War I - from 1914 to 1918, fought in Europe. Great Britain, France, Russia, the United States, and their allies were on one side. Germany, Austria-Hungary, and their allies were on the other side.

WEB SITES

To learn more about gun history and development, visit ABDO Publishing Company online. Web sites about gun history and development are featured on our Book Links page. These links are routinely monitored and updated to provide the most current information available.

www.abdopublishing.com

INDEX

A

accuracy 10, 13, 17, 18, 27
ammunition 4, 8, 9, 10, 12, 16, 17, 18, 20, 22, 23, 25
arquebus 12, 13, 14
automatic weapon 26, 27

B

Bacon, Roger 7
Beretta, Bartolomeo 25
Berthold, Black 4, 6, 29
black powder 4, 6, 7, 8, 9, 10, 12
Browning, John Moses 26

C

cannon 8, 9, 10, 12, 16, 20
Capone, Al 26
cartridge 22, 23
Coalition to Stop Gun Violence 28

D

decoration 24, 25
Dillinger, John 26
duels 19

F

flintlock 15, 22

G

gunpowder 4, 6, 14, 17, 22, 23

H

hand cannon 10, 12
hunting 17

K

Kollner, Gaspard 16

M

matchlock 13, 14
materials 8, 10, 14, 15, 17, 20, 22, 23, 24
military 10, 14, 17, 20, 25, 27, 28
musket 13, 14, 16

N

National Rifle Association 28
Norton, John 20

P

percussion lock 22, 23
pistol 18, 19
primer 12, 22, 23

R

revolver 18
rifle 17, 20

S

Second Amendment 28
semiautomatic weapon 26
shotgun 17

T

Thompson submachine gun 26, 27

W

wheel lock 14, 15